OUR OWN HIGH SCHOOL, AL WARQA'A

Our Own High School, Al Warqa'a, is a GEMS school created in 2005 as a single shift facility for boys of 'Our Own English High School, Dubai' which was established in Bastakiya in 1968. 'Our Own' Al Warqa'a shares the same vision, ethos, and work culture that has given the parent school its laudable presence. 'Our Own' Al Warqa'a now has 4,700 students and 218 teachers. The school is well-recognized for the quality of its academic achievements and the service it provides to students and parents. Our educational priorities are based on current trends that affect education globally, and on the shared leadership and management agenda that is consciously emerging across GEMS schools.

Our Own High School, Al Warqa'a encourages ambition and acknowledges potential, educating students to become critical thinkers and compassionate citizens, whilst attaining academic distinction within a creative and supportive environment.

English Language
Our Own Verses
(Anthology of Poems)
Compiled by
Asim Fawz Jaleel, Kavya Malav Mehta

Published in November 2023
by Decan Imprint Publishing Co.
Reg. Off: Sharjah Publishing City
Free Zone Sharjah, UAE.
Phone: 00971-551830334
Email : decanimprint@gmail.com

Cover Design :Aromal O.P, Prasanth Mangad
Printed at
Manipal Technologies Ltd

07/23-24/Sl.No.07/150/18.6 NS
ISBN 978-93-94472-64-8

OUR OWN VERSES

Compiled by:
Asim Fawz Jaleel
Kavya Malav Mehta

Decan Imprint

THE PAW TEAM

Aasim Fawz Jaleel– Head of Operations (Left), Ms. Valin Rita– Teacher Coordinator (Middle), Kavya Malav Mehta– Head of Technology (Right)

ACKNOWLEDGEMENTS

We express our heartfelt gratitude to our Principal, Dr. Anjuly Murthy for her continuous motivation.

We also thank our Vice Principal, Mr. Kapil Chaudhary for his ever-extended support in taking up this initiative at school level.

A million thanks wouldn't suffice for our Head of the Senior School, Mrs. Anitha Nair for her constant guidance in making this initiative a success.

We forever remain grateful to our teacher coordinator, Ms. Valin Rita Patel for her expertise and valuable insights.

Our special thanks to Sri Varshini Senguttuvan and Vishesh Shukla for digital interfaces and visual idea.

A big shout out to all the poets across the school for their remarkable pieces.

Last but not at all the least, we thank Dr. Kassim Rawther and 'Kairali Publications for making this dream come true.

Aasim Fawz Jaleel

OUR OWN PAWISTS!

FROM THE PRINCIPAL'S DESK!

We at "Our Own High School' encourage our children to dream, aspire, and strive to seek triumph. Thus, we embark each one of them on the vehicle of education, steering them through a pleasant and joyful journey of self-exploration, by providing unique opportunities to express themselves in varied forms.

Poetry is one such form of powerful expression. It is a rich experience that not only helps students improve their linguistic skills and communication but also stimulates their creative thinking.

'OOHS PAW CHALLENGE' is an ingenious platform, exclusively initiated and designed by our senior students. It hosts a collection of around 120 poems, witnessing a compilation of varied themes and ideas, setting a stage for budding poets to venture outside their classrooms.

It gives me immense pleasure and pride as the Principal of Our Own High School to witness the birth of 40 poets and their miraculous writings. 'Our Own Verses' presents a plethora of poems that will undoubtedly lead you through a memorable experience.

I congratulate our young writers for their innovative pieces and pray that their young igniting minds continue to foster natural curiosity, imagination, and invention.

Best Wishes,
Dr. Anjuly Murthy
Principal
Our Own High School, Dubai

MESSAGE FROM HEAD OF SENIOR SCHOOL

Dear Readers,

The first edition of PAW -Poem A Week, is a captivating compilation of poems created by our talented student body over the past 1 Term. These verses showcase the incredible creativity and diverse perspectives within our school community.

Each poem in this collection truly reflects the passion and imagination that thrives among our students.

I believe that poetry has the power to connect, inspire, and provoke thought, and this compilation is a testament to the artistic talent that defines our school.

I extend my heartfelt thanks to the dedicated student team who brought this initiative to life.

As we continue to nurture creativity within our school, let this compilation be a reminder of the endless possibilities that await each of you. Your words have the power to change the world, and I have no doubt that you will continue to make a meaningful impact through your artistic endeavors.

Congratulations to all the featured poets.

I look forward to witnessing the continued growth and success of our talented poets.

With Best Wishes!
Anitha Nair
Head of Senior School

Creating and organizing an event can be a challenging yet immensely rewarding experience. "PAW CHALLENGE" was more than just an event; it was a labor of love and a testament to our passion for poems. It required meticulous planning and coordination. It was obviously not a one-man's job. The invaluable contributions of our team, volunteers, and attendees played a crucial role in making the event a resounding success. The power of poetry lies in its ability to inspire, heal, and provoke thought. "PAW CHALLENGE" did just that. "PAW CHALLENGE" is not just an event; it is a celebration of the human spirit and the capacity of words to illuminate our innermost thoughts and emotions. As we appreciate this remarkable gathering of poets and poetry enthusiasts, we recognize that it is a testament to the enduring power of language. The event stands as a reminder that, through poetry, we can connect, empathize, and find solace in the beauty of the written word.

Congratulations to all the poets and thank you for your contributions!

Best Regards
Kavya Malav Mehta
Head of Technology
PAW Challenge

As a small poet
From a small town
I too saw some small dreams

And I didn't realize when they changed,
Because back when I was in eighth
I wanted to be read
In every school
Every book
And every page.

But today
This one page's all I have
But I glimmer with pride
For what's following is what I carved.

It is a dream come true
One I'll never forget
The PAW Challenge
With 120 poems and 40 poets.

We tried new themes
And learned new forms
Took a break from school
And let our thoughts roam

We gave them a chance
To speak it out
Reciting and writing
New poets were born.

This idea occurred
From a poet I'd see
Sarah Kay
And her lovely poetries

Now the book is published
And all I can see
Is the smiles of the boys
That told me I'd succeed.

I wish the boys all the best
And to keep writing
For layman or rest
For tonight you turn
Published poet indeed
So keep writing
And let your pen speak!

Best Regards
Aasim Fawz Jaleel
Head of Operations
PAW Challenge

GLOSSARY OF THEMES

'OOHS PAW CHALLENGE' is a unique poetry challenge initiated by the students at the senior school, hosted for the students of grades 6 to 12. The term 'PAW' is the abbreviation for 'Poem a Week' which is the modified version of the internationally celebrated 'Poem a Day Challenge.' PAW Challenge celebrates the collection of over 120 poems written by around 45 student poets and proudly presents a plethora of eloquent poetry.

The OOHS PAW challenge ran for a course of 4 months providing ample time and breaks between studies, exams, and even vacations to the poets for carving their beautiful verses. Over the course of 4 months, we have covered 6 topics, 3 forms of poetry and have encouraged the poets to come up with their very own form of poetry.

The topics covered -

Week 1

Once While I Was Walking Alone

Week 2

An Acrostic Poem on A Special Someone

(An acrostic is a poem composition in which the first letter of each new line spells out a word, message, or the alphabet.)

Week 3

Seniors - Beauty Lies in The Eye of The Beholder

Juniors- A poem to my future/past self

Week 4

A Deam That Is Yet to Be Dreamt

Week 5

Seniors - Concrete Poetry

Concrete poetry creates a particular shape or form on the page that echoes the poem's message. This form of poetry uses layout and spacing to emphasize certain themes, and they sometimes take the shape of their subjects. For instance, a poem about the moon may have a decidedly crescent shape.

Juniors - Clerihew

(Clerihews are four lines long

Line one ends with a person's name.

The first two lines rhyme together.

The last two lines rhyme together.

The poem MUST be funny)

Week 6

Seniors - A Desi Household

Juniors - A mistake I'd Like to Repeat

Week 7

CREATE YOUR OWN FORM OF POETRY!

Writers inside

NAVEEN BALAKRISHNAN - 12 C

ONCE WHILE I WAS WALKING ALONE

A REMINISCENT REMINDER

One fine dawn, before the daybreak
Alone strolled a lad, then so young.
A decade ago, in the midst of smog
Endured an enigma of sheer oblivion.

Passing the sea, a thought in him twinkled,
"Why am I here?", his head tangled.
"Where do I belong?", his heart muddled.
In due perplexion, his hands huddled.

Clueless, paused the boy to think,
"Whence have I come from?", He asked in a blink.
He theorized in his pristine fantasy,
Of epics and myths, engulfed in majesty.

But innocence is transient, and so was his tale,
For he has changed; now a grown male.
He resides in me, as I take a lone walk,
And ponder in vain, "Am I the same?
 The sea is immortal and so is the path.
The self is however not so gullible.
Burning the hypothesis of fictional fables,
The mind is mortal and so is my wrath

I reminisce the past as if it were a miracle,
"Am I an old and pristine fiction?"
"Are my theories of life just fabled?"
"Does life offer none to its poignant children?"

Clueless, paused I to think,
"Whence have I come from?", I asked in a blink
But realized the pangs of undue mortality
As life, now dwells in regret and poignancy

As I take this woeful walk,
My soul; embellished with rough stones,
And a tale that once lost its tranquil tones,
Now debates this mythical fabric.

ACROSTIC POEM
A Son's Oath

Mighty Sailed thee across the endearing ocean of life.
Omnipresent, battled thy spine-tingling shadows.
Traversing the ethereal sea of material existence,
Harnessing the harpooned hogs of heaven with grace.
Eternal; lies your spirit and soul in solace.
Reminiscent; lies your enigma, amidst our sunken shade.

BEAUTY LIES IN THE EYE OF THE BEHOLDER
BEAUTIFYING MYSTICS

Beautified in her mystic banquet,
Bridal stood she, amidst the hassle,
Spectating, spit out in vanquished sass,
Critical, draped an entire blanket.

The eyes speculated, not one, but many,
Fabricating opinions on her undulating looks.
The beholder has availed to his aristocratic fantasy,
Diminishing the stricken to her depth-deepening crooks.

Ugly, one proclaimed,
Impoverished, another claimed.
But then arose her mother's spirit,
Lauding her daughter's beauty, so implicit.

The beholder can bribe his eerie, vile brain,
For beauty lies in the eyes of this beholder.
Society is known, only to self-proclaim,
But beauty lies in the eyes of the beholder.

A DREAM THAT IS YET TO BE DREAMT
UNDREAMT DREAMS

The veil of slumber lightly befell,
Upon the pearls of the human face;
As the nucleus took a gentle dive;
Deep, down the dearth of blossoming weavery.

Traversing to the treacherous trenches,
Engulfed in an enigma of untold ecstasy;
Shutting down to renew and recharge,
And restart its overdue processor base.

Fantasy, histo,ry and mirage prevailed,
Unraveling the mysteries of the dwindled brain;
As the past, present and future swindled,
Realism fell into a dreadful miracle.

All but one sole fragment remained,
Curtailed in the backrooms, waiting for its turn;
Yet to cross the path of oblivion,
Who knows what secrets this one withholds?

CONCRETE POETRY DESI HOUSEHOLD

The Omnipresent Ocean

By Naveen Balakrishnan, 12C

Calmly flowing through its Cerulean canopy

Tranquil, engaging in over-powering swirls

Encasing ecosystems, amidst its dearth;

Engraving existence, within its peripheries.

Beaming with omnipresence,

Exhibiting exuberance;

Expliciting extravagance,

Gleaming with pure lustre.

Sly and enigmatic, Dashingly daring.

He lets out a shriek:

S
P
L
O
O
S
H
:

But thriving lives have disappeaed?!

off to a far-off village.

I pray they find solace there...

DREAMY DESI DELIGHTS

Deep down under viridescent canopies,
Resting amidst the southeastern mangroves,
Majestically stood a lone duplex,
Embraced by reeds, rail, and roadways.

The world outside our corners is wild.
On the inside though, it lies quite sublime.
Engulfed in the invigorating aroma of Southern Petrichor,
My Desi household always stays alight.

Not a single day can rest,
Without a fulfilling mixture of curd rice and potato fry.
Tingling our taste buds with undue tranquility,
A home-made touch is the true cherry-on-top.

A visit to the temple is a noble practice,
Admiring the architectural marvels of the ancient.
In silenced chambers we deeply pray,
A meditative aura engulfs the atmosphere.

Festival bounds family and friends,
As old nightmares disperse eternally,
 New values rise in the air,
Waving the love-bound flag of oneness.

Aunties gossip in exciting secrecy,
As uncles politicize dreadful laws,

But all this ends in a gala of celebration,
As the authentic household returns to normalcy.

Grandma's fairy-tales engulf the air,
As grandpa displays his historical bravery.
Mother's hands cook up new delicacies,
Together functioning as a true Desi household.

The sound of the rail echoes at an instant,
Rhythmic, matching the beats of the mortar.
The pleasant sight of the passing train,
Vibrates in resonance to the clash of the stones.

The train takes with itself; decades of memories,
Keeping alive its everyday grandeur.
Though it's whistle fades in the distance,
The memories of that house resonate vividly.

 Water fills the majestic tank,
As it washes off the dirt from soiled fabric.
Drying the sparkling saris at noon,
A bird's arrival brings immense grace.

As dusk befalls the never-ending horizon,
The talk for dinner rises into discussion.
A hearty meal gives a hearty mind,
As the soul rests into deep slumber.

Deep down under viridescent canopies,
Resting amidst the southeastern mangroves,
Majestically stood a lone duplex,
Now, drifting away into unknown oblivion

NEW FORM OF POETRY

This short poem is comprised of numerous couplets put together. the significance of each couplet is about how the first line is quite long whereas the second is comparatively short. another key feature is how both lines contrast each other. The use of the names of poetic devices also describes certain real-life issues. the poem starts with a totally literary-related idea, supporting the composer's use of oxymorons but also talks about the same use of oxymorons making it difficult for readers to comprehend the poem's meaning. over the next 3 couplets, present-day power-hungry politicians take place of the writers, bombarding the readers(common folk) with fake promises and incomprehensible vows in the form of litotes. thereby, this poetry form highlights a political issue through totally unrelated literacy-related words, while also utilizing the ancient method of couplets to convey a strong societal ideology, representing both sides of the same coin.

OMINOUS OXYMORONS

Combined contrasts open doors of creativity,
Ruining readers' minds.
Widely blooming through poems and plays,
Watchers wail in agony.
The volcano of ideas erupts with oxymorons,
Terribly troubling the tribes.
When power-hungry politicians spill their antithesis,
Dwellers drown in litotes.

DALVIN THOMAS - 12A

ACROSTIC POEM

A Tribute to Martyrs

Mindless of the pain we face,
Around us the enemies gather.
Remember us as we bid farewell for
This journey we take beyond the world.
Ye countrymen, may ye live and prosper!

Rays of sun shall we see no more.

SOORYA VIDHU DINIL -12B

ACROSTIC POEM

First Person to Truly Understand Me
Relation Not by Blood
In The Darkest of Nights
Even When All Hell in Sight
Now And Forever with Me
Deep Bonds Cherished both
Scarfs That Safely Hold Me

AADHI NARAYAN – 12A
RIVER OF LIFE

As rugged or smooth the flow of Life may Lie,
And as far as the perfection of the waves may be undefined,
Through the ages of time as far as dust,
And through periods of provoked changed,
We found perfection in our ancestors and us,
The beauty of complexity that has never been paged,
Like a mouse let loose running among its cage,
It inspired many auth to be what many may not see,
We just share our paintings of words page by page,
As long as the story of our theatre may produce a past,
The curtains to this play will forever last.

DESI HOUSEHOLD
VERANDAS

The halls of mischief and echoing cries,
And where our childhood once resides,
Filled with memories of happiness and tears,
And of the days our grades were feared,
The days of chatting with loved once we know we miss,
And of the bloodlines lost to the mist,
Now we grew out of these halls of relentless emotions.
To one with none at all,
The halls of adulthood were never the same,
And all I will remember is the memories of the
verandas in which we used to play.

ARYAN GUPTA - 12B

WHY DID I LET THE TIME?

"Looking at the Clock,
Time passing by
Excitement commands,
The wait goes by
I enjoy, enjoy, enjoy
Build a Moment with the Beyond,
The Clock strikes bye?
How?
Regret I have, Rejoice I don't
Why did that time pass by?
I ask myself
Inside lies in the captures I took,
But look!
Whether Good or Bad, Happy or Sad, Memory or
Tragedy,
Life moves the Book"

SHREECHARAN ASHOKKUMAR- 11E

ONCE WHILE I WAS WALKING ALONE

Once it was such
That I was walking alone
With my head in the clouds
And humming in a baritone

And so on I walked
A silent one
In the chorus of many a moan
Thousands of bodies – left and right

And yet I walked alone
With unnatural happiness
My brain did wander
In the stretches of paradise

Of whose I was the creator
A manufactured paradise t'was,
A dream to distract,
From the greatest of distress

A dream to separate,
The body and soul
A dream to formulate,
Pleasure tainted with artificiality

But suddenly, blinding light entered
The recesses of my brain
From the illusion of lies, I woke
And so, my eyes opened again
 Blackness crashed down,
And so did my soul
A faltering step- 'Death!' I thought
With a heart very whole

But an arm clasped me
And from left and right,
So did thousands more
I rose, now slow, now sure

I truly woke
Then I saw
Then I knew
I was not alone anymore

ACROSTIC POEM
A Question of Ability

A thought, it struck me once, a
Query t'was, and desired an answer.
'Undreds of lyrical pieces
Effortlessly I'd read
Sparing the most thoughts for
The author of the ode.
In the golden glory of these creators, the query I'd had:
O' can I or can I not, ever
'Ngender a verse of exquisite art?
On these terms I did start
Following the path of the poetic heart
As it is now, a long way I've come,
Bygone days spent in creation
In hope that I shall find place as a
Lewis, Frost, or Tagore of the contiguous gen.
I daresay, my best I've done yet
There's more to travel, but this can be said:
Yearning for my success, a question had created.

BEAUTY LIES IN THE EYE OF THE BEHOLDER
BEAUTY

'Beauty'
A word of extreme complexity
One that can be used to appease,
But never to contrast

A word that can be used to delight
But never to collate
For what is one's treasure
May be another's trash

Though a word frequently used,
To its true meaning, is shown ignorance.
For beauty, it's not materialistic
With perspective, it does vary.

What may cause a gardener's brow to crease,
May be an artist's masterpiece.
And what is one's monotone,
May be another's life in color.
If one looks the right way,
Even a dried leaf is beauty in itself

Oh, to speak of the multitude of mindsets
In this world of views,
It'll take me long, that isn't a ruse.
But the moral, it shall be quicker
'Beauty is in the eye of the beholder"

A DREAM THAT IS YET TO BE DREAMT

A Dream not Yet Dreamt
A Dream not yet dreamt'
What is such a thing?
Is it an inexistent fantasy?
Or an elusive reality?

My thoughts speak as thus:
An art not on canvas,
An unspoken word,
Are the same
as a dream unexpressed.

For that is what it is.
Unborn, latent
In the recesses of minds of many, it is present
A figment of our thought
An impalpable object
with a purpose unfulfilled
Yes, that's what it is.

And yet it roils with power.
it contains the potential
to create empires of grandeur
that changes fate itself.

For, in its greatest form, it manipulates.
mankind's greatest tool
And one's heart it does send,
towards his true path's end
For within, it awakens desire.

CONCRETE POETRY!

<u>THE APOSTROPHE</u>

Oh those ones,

Who drive me out
Let me see you take me down
But you'll see that you suffer with me gone
The one who uses me improperly: You! Yes, you!
The one who deems me to be unnecessary: You, still You!
Elaborate will you not? On my apparently 'useless' existence.
The great ignorant who thinks that, of all, he is the most wise,
You are leading your people with yourself to danger in disguise
My death: the mother of many communicative misconceptions.
Without me around, a text: 'Boy**'s** life in the greatest of perils'
May soon become such: '**Boys**   lives in danger very grave!
Without me in existence,   A property which's your's
May become   a soon unclaimed orphan
You! I question you now
Do you really intend to
Destroy your language
Due to laziness of use?
Do you truly intend to
Convey what you do
- not ever wish to?
My protectors,
Now inexistent.
So free advice,
I give you.
Let me stay

Only then will you.

ADITYA KADHI -11C

ONCE WHILE I WAS WALKING ALONE

Once while I was walking alone,
Lost in thoughts, with a heart full of stone,
I heard a voice, sweet and loveful
whispering in my ears, soul, and mind

Son, the voice said, do not despair, I am with you,
always there, in your each and every step breath
I am life and I am death

I am light that guides your way
The truth which will give you satisfaction
I am love that fills your heart
The wisdom that sets you apart

The road may be wide and long
But you must remain steadfast and strong
Have faith in me and trust my will
find love, find happiness find your career
you will find me everywhere

so, walk with me and you shall see,
A life full of love, joy and harmony
Remember me in every situation
I will remember you throughout the life and take away your all
sorrow

Follow my words, my path, my expression.
I will give you eternal peace, enlightenment and career
Remember me, your heart would be fill of love
I am life and I am the death

ACROSTIC POEM

Trusted confident, my rock and support,
Endlessly giving, your love is my fort,
Journeying together, hand in hand,
And bond unbreakable, forever grand,
Lifelong gratitude, you truly understand.

Thankful for the sacrifices you've made,
Ever selfless, with a heart unsawed
Joyful memories, etched deep within,
A mother's love, a treasure to begin,
Loving you deeply, my heart shall ever win.

Tejal, like a guiding star's soft glow,
Elevating spirits, making us whole,
Jovial and serene, like the Yamuna's flow,
A mother's love, a divine halo,
Lovingly nurturing, helping us grow

In your love, we taste the nectar of devotion,
sharing the life knowledge, spreading the notion,
Unconditional love, a guiding light,
Nourishing our spirits, from day to night

YASER ZAMAN LABEEB - 11A

ONCE WHILE I WAS WALKING ALONE
A Walk of Losses

I remember a time, long ago
never felt lonely while walking alone
Surrounded by birds, puddles and bushes of jasmine and rose
And the thing which I held dear to most
The one who took care of me
Looming over the landscape, a singular tree
With all this, I continued to walk forward, Dwindling bushes,
muddier puddles and
not a single bird,
But as I progressed this now dull path, The tree was still there.
And because of that I did not care, oh I really didn't care
I now walk in a desolate landscape with no tree, and with
nobody longer beside me.
I slug along this path I do not want to see the end of,
I stagger along the uncaring path which will offer nothing but a
cruel send off,
A brilliant idea it would be to stop walking and have a peaceful
peek of the
aftermath.
Nothing's good ever happened to me in this cruddy path...

..... Besides for the birds,
Besides for the puddles,
Besides for the bushes of jasmine and rose
And the thing which I held dear to most,
No longer looming over the landscape.....
.....A singular tree Which took care of me.

ACROSTIC POEM
One More time, Once Again

Regretful for not spending enough time with you
And hopeful that we will meet again
Jester man you are leaving so soon
Early it is, please don't let it end
So I can collect more memories of you and I
Hyperman of the ages, please don't say bye

Fabulous friend you encourage me too much
Really great listener, I wanna talk about you for a change
In desperate situations, you always come in clutch
Embittered I am not anymore, I've accepted that things won't
be the same
No! I won't forget you, I love you a lot my friend
Do hang out with me please, one more time, once again

BEAUTY LIES IN THE EYE OF THE BEHOLDER
Mrs. Raccoon

Mrs. Raccoon loves trash,
I just don't get it,
Don't mean to be brash,
But there's so much better than it.

A good combo meal,
isn't enough to satisfy
its preferred in the garbage,
let her put it inside.

Some of the world's greatest treasures,
ehhhhhh that's kind of mediocre,
it isn't really waste,
nor does it have a smelly odor?

She's coming over dinner,
Needn't put feast for ages,
She'll inspect it thoroughly,
N put in much of her garbage.

The house is clean enough,
She comes inside with a smile,
I already know what she's about to do,
I can see it from a mile.

She takes my belongings,
And stuffs it in her bag,
She calls it "decoration",
That's enough, I'll finally make her understand.

I sit her down in the couch,
Preparing to deliver the message,
She's now taking my socks,
Declares it beautiful when it's garbage.

"It seems our eyes differ,
Well, yours absolutely sucks,
I say we should part ways pal,
Goodbye and best of luck."

I hear a sound of anger,
And rocket raccoon ran,
I look out of my window,
Idiot's distracted by a garbage can.

Mrs. Raccoon loves garbage,
I just don't get it.
It seems like I never will,
But I can live with it.

A DREAM THAT IS YET TO BE DREAMT
Insomnia

Don't go into that room,
He's awake,
His eyes are closed?
Well, it's still fake.

Every night, he stares,
Staring with his eyes closed,
He looks deep at the abyss,
Wishing for a slight chance he dozed.
The madman shifts slightly,
Changing his style,
But he's still so far from rest,
He still has to sleep a mile.

He's bent, he's standing,
He's now laying,
Doesn't matter how he sleeps,
He'll be awake until 7 AM.

Next morning, when he comes down,
Don't ask how he slept,
He'll be cranky and sarcastic,
Claims he dreamt a dream which hadn't been dreamt.
Confused you will be, and that's fine,
No need to derive sense,
His dream to dream never fulfilled,
Stuck he is, dreaming a dream never been dreamt

NATHAN JOHN MUDAY - 11 E

ONCE WHILE I WAS WALKING ALONE

Once while I was walking alone,
I heard a voice say to me...
"Why do you take this lonely road,
When there is someone to be - with"

I didn't know who was talking,
Not caring to look around.
Because I knew the one who was saying this,
Would not be found.

"You have so much with you,
but you choose to leave it all.
You can't see beyond your problem.
To your mind in thrall"

I continued walking still,
Understanding what this voice was conveying,
I chose not to listen,
But I couldn't help all the memories replaying.

"You have to learn to see the good in the bad,
Life isn't always a bed of roses.
Sure, you've suffered a lot,
But that doesn't mean you have to end up enclosed in!'

The voice continued on reasoning,
With each step I took I started questioning.
Was what I was doing necessary?
And then I could see the end, the distance lessening.

Now wait, this is where you must pay attention,
Because what you do next cannot be undone there is only
prevention.
Do not make a choice if you see through you will only regret,
The damage has been done but you can choose to forget."

I stood there for a long moment and then I gave up and sat
down crying,
All the different emotions I experienced - I tried fighting.
But the only thing I wanted to do then was to be grateful,
For the voice that stopped an ending so very painful.

In mental exhaustion and with the energy I had which was few,
I slowly managed to whisper the words 'Thank You
I needed to get everything together, after saying that line,
And I knew I possessed the strength to do that because that
voice... was mine.

CONCRETE POETRY!

PLASTIC

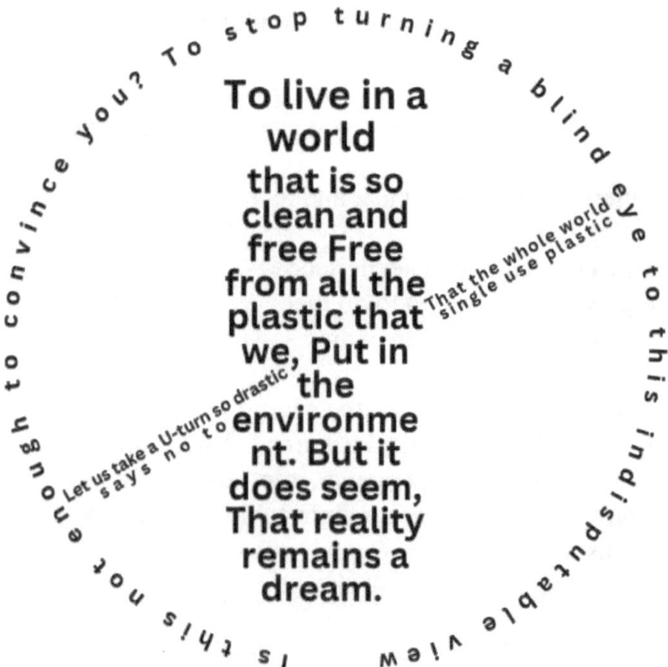

ADVAIT MADHAVAN - 11C

ONCE WHILE I WAS WALKING ALONE

The Little Sparrow
Alone I walked under a quiet night, Unaware.
of the sudden flush of despair,
that would shake me hard,
Leave me scared.

The little sparrow haunted me endless,
As it lay on the street lifeless.
I stared at it with a broken heart,
As a thought within tore me apart.

Will I die the same way?
Nobody to mourn that day?
Lying dead tranquil,
As onlookers passed languid.

But I have come to realize,
For her death did the nature mourn,
For her death did this poem mourn,
For her death did I mourn.

VISHESH SHUKLA - 11B

ONCE WHILE I WAS WALKING ALONE

For once I had been on my own,
Walking a path, I had yet to explore,
On an unfamiliar path, trembling with fear,
It was about time I had to veer,
Quite an interesting place I am set to throne,
for once I was to walk alone.

Once upon a time, my feet knew only play,
Skipping over stones and chasing the day.
The world was wide, and life was sweet,
with every moment a new discovery to meet.

But as the sun began to set on my youth,
I felt the weight of time, the pull of truth.
And so, I set out on this solitary walk,
O find a path that no one else had thought to talk.

I walked through the rocky trails,
With every step, my courage failed,
Yet still I pushed through doubts and pain,
Determined not to lose again.

And then I saw a flower bright,
Its petals dancing in the light,
And in its beauty, I found grace,
A glimpse of childhood's pure embrace.

But now I see the path was one,
That both sides of life had overcome,
And though it may be hard at times,
The journey is true to its design.
So, I will walk with courage bold,
And embrace each step,
both new and old,
For once while I was walking all alone...

ACROSTIC POEM

 Keen eyes full of mischief and fun,
unleashing joy with every wag,
keep my spirits from ever sag.
Unpredictable, you bring surprise.
unleashing laughter, my heart flies.
unbreakable bond, like a precious child.
Knocking over things with a wagging tail,
Your presence never fails.
kind and loving, through and through,
keeps my heart warm, just like you.
Unconditional love, pure and true,
unleashing happiness, it's all you do.
forever grateful, for you I'm smitten,
KUKU, my furry friend, never bitten.

A DREAM THAT IS YET TO BE DREAMT

Dreaming vividly, reality feels untrue,
Within, my inner self comes into View.
In the realm of dreams, my spirit takes flight,
Exploring landscapes where imagination ignites.

Through the mist of dreams, I wander and roam,
Where illusions dance in a world of their own.
Dreams unfold like petals of a vibrant flower,
Guiding me closer to my destined power.

Within dreams' embrace, solace I find,
Where aspirations awaken in my mind.
A dream that has yet to be dreamt,
Unfolding its magic, yet unmet.

DESI HOUSEHOLD

In each Desi household, a sacred art,
Where spices and love blend, right from the heart.
A kitchen alive with fragrance and flair,
Where a mother's love weaves stories to share.

From cumin's warm hug to turmeric's embrace,
Each spice tells a tale of a comforting place.

In the pot, a symphony of flavors unites,
Crafted by Mom, with pure love and insight.

A pinch of nostalgia, a dash of care,
She stirs in devotion, a fragrance to bear.
Every dish tells a story, a memory so sweet,
From her hands to our hearts, it's a delightful feat.

In the heart of the home, where memories reside,
A mother's love and spices coincide.
Each meal a masterpiece, each bite a treat,
A Desi household's love story, oh, so sweet.
"Spice-Infused Love" dances in the air,
A connection to roots, beyond compare.
With each delectable dish, a bond is sown,
In the heart of Desi homes, forever known...

SAHIL MOHAMMED - 11A

ONCE WHILE I WAS WALKING ALONE

Once while I was walking alone,
I was just staring at my phone,
The world felt completely monotone,
Boredom strike-d my bone.

Then I looked at the sky and the ground,
Nothing interesting around I found,
There was not a single sound,
Only me and the faded background.

The road I walked showed no end,
Yet I continued with no hands to support or lend,
The only things that didn't perish
Were the memories I fondly cherish.

SRAVAN VINOD - 10 N

ONCE WHILE I WAS WALKING ALONE

When Alone on a Stroll
 On my way to the obscure
I strolled across piles of green
Betwixt the frond
Appeared a flock of entozoons

Hundreds of worms bequeathed a grin
Seeing myself all alone
Though just a musing
It gave my heart a thump

On and on I plodded the meadow
Dwelling on my life every step
Loneliness clutched me tight.
Until I almost broke

Then I glanced at the sun
Unaided the mighty orb stood alone.
it lit the glob solus.
Along with it my road

It proffered the will.
To walk till the end
And nevermore did I rue my entity.
I continued the walk now knowing where to go.

ACROSTIC POEM

Midst of darkness, when shadows seemed deep,
You stood giving light, guiding me out of the keep.

Magnanimous you were before every slip.
Oceans of love that flowed from your heart uplifts me
whenever I trip
That way that you make me chuckle when tears drip caused
me to feel
Hale and certain that darkness won't crack that seal.
Every fresh day, my admiration for you grows and grows.
Reverence I have, for the strength your presence bestows.

BEAUTY LIES IN THE EYE OF THE BEHOLDER

Not By the Eye

I've seen Oysters by the shore.
Thrown away by some men.
Piled and perceived worthless
The host of a priceless gem

I've seen an Oleander blossom.
Charming every glance
Yet a leaf off the radiant bloom
Makes a man meet his marker.

The sight your orbs catch.
Is hardly a fleck of a droplet.
Of the vast ocean
Beyond the grin

A DREAM THAT IS YET TO BE DREAMT

The earliest beam of sunshine
touched my ravenous form.
and then arouse my bones.
at the fear of being lashed
A glance I gave to the left and right.
Where are my brothers?
Where are my sisters?
I bawled to the shed of hay.

With a broken heart I had to progress
my penurious legs darted out of the shed.
fearful of the whip
to hear petrifying yelp
that caused me to rush towards the source of sound.
across pasture, towards the obscure
and there I found my kin.
soaked in blood lying nearly stock-still.

I couldn't help but weep.
as I watched my master whip maa
I was impotent before those eyes of savagery.

relishing the sin
I did nothing but stroll to the field.
where I had to labor till the dark
even though my agonizing scarred back.
pushed me to my limits I kept at it.

After the gleaming moon gave a shine
I mused looking at the crescent.
dwelling on my unfortunate entity
as I put the hoe to rest
I then sauntered towards the poky shed.
where my siblings were resting
after the vengeance they received
just for sleeping a little longer the previous day.

What crime have I committed?
What sin did I commit for this misery filled being?
My innocent mind pondered.
not knowing who would secure the next lash.
as I dozed that cold night dreaming of having a blanket
I was perplexed by the thought that why my master.
whom I consider my father doesn't have the warmth.
to lend me a piece of cloth to ward off the cold.

Though it seems nothing but fantasy
This was the harsh reality.
of the daily life of a famished slave
under the white paramountcy heretofore
I was one of millions of wretched men.
forced to be oxen.
until we broke the chain
walking towards a bright life

57

So, my friends, savor liberty to the fullest
Cherish even the paltry things in life.
Spread your wings to a future.
Where all beings are treated the same
Where the world advances like never before
when equality becomes that stupendous dream
that most of earth has never dreamt before

CONCRETE POEM
THE HEAVENLY PEAK

To

whom

does the brightness

of heaven belong? Who owns the

splendor of the sky? O! There she is

Within the arrive of Indrakil the king of mountains

welcomes the sun. Among the azure rivers and cloisters

Towering milky waterfalls, charming every glance the snow capped

giant Lies in the lap of Mother Nature. The land of prosperity and diversity

radiant with colour in every fleck Is home to the majestic peak, Kanchenjunga.

A DESI HOUSEHOLD

A Desi Hive

The land where diversity thrives.
is the cradle of the human race.
Within the august state are Desi hives
brimming with hues that do amaze.
and here we are to embrace.

The oldest of radios plays the newest of music,
oldest of eyes examines the newest of prints.
A tidy floor wiped daily by the oldest tunic.
remains so neat and uncluttered that you can't sprint.
More than worthy for a squint.

While the mother tugs water from the bore
The sister and gran stir the curry.
Condiments flow from their hands to the fore.
The dyads remain buried in hurry.
A Trembling and quivering kitchen we leave behind.

The man of the house slashes the green.
to supplement the savor.
In the pots of mud that can be seen
are companions of the flavor.
All and sundry have to labor.
The aroma of curries pervades the air,
the delectable Sadhya fills the table.
The words of wisdom from the elders feel so rare.
Peace and calmness fortify the house and stable.
"A lovely place" remains the label.

NEW FORM OF POETRY
Ironic free verse form of poetry -

Irony is a form of figure of speech in which the person delivering the ironic statement says something which is completely opposite to what they mean or what the reality of the situation is.
Here the soldier who is seriously hit by bullets is enjoying the environment albeit the agony. He feels happy to know his friend is beside him with even more bullet wounds. He curses the medic who saved his life, instead of appreciating the care he received in the shelter he craves to go back to where he was shot down. This is the opposite to the reality of the situation.
The poem also conveys a hidden message of how beautiful the world would be if there wasn't any violence and destruction. It tells the reader to pursue the path of non-violence and peace. A world without any wars will be stupendous.

A flare of muzzle flash from nowhere

Amidst a battle, a soldier we find.
unaware of the flare of muzzle flash from nowhere
until when hit by the bullets of hatred.
While falling towards the earth he gazes
the beautiful earth around him.

The birds chirp as daylight turns to afternoon.
A beautiful flock of flowers clutches him as he plummets.

A cold breeze welcomes his delighted mind.
Peacefulness fills his entity.
He finally cherishes his being.
He casts a peek to the right.
to find his best friend lying beside him
With a blissful grin
He points out the charming marvels of nature.
A radiant day lay before them.

Soon he imparts the truth to his pal,
the two bullets resting in his midriff.
His friend chuckles in response and then reveals.
the four bullets that quivered into him.
A short moment of silence that followed ended by a burst of
laughter.

Alas, a medic approaches the wounded men.
lugging them away towards a shelter
Away from the blossom, away from the sun
away from the zephyr and from the blue.
Now reclining in a poky shack.

Curses the soldiers at the medic with dejected hearts.
for divesting them of the exquisite nature.
They thirst for a tranquil environment.
Albeit the agony, they ponder.
the brood of losing that sight pains more

ABHAY RAJESH -10N

ONCE WHILE I WAS WALKING ALONE
Walking Through Forlorn Alone

Strolling through the fallen leaves of orange, red and yellow,
The chirps of the myna, like the colors mellow.
The trees that wave at me, while I roam,
Whisper quietly, I walk alone.

I make my path ahead, for nothing drawn,
Passing thicker into the woods, forlorn.
Trapped amongst the bare who mock,
Takes hold of me, from the undone walk.

Cries of despair echo through the distance.
Finally unshackled, from vengeance.
The strong winds and the dark hinder,
I make my path ahead, while I wither.

Toiling up my path, while on my own.
Enduring the hard stones that were thrown.
I go on, not knowing what lies ahead,
Wiped all the tears that were shed.

A walk that started colorful and bright,
Turned the tables, grey with fright.
On foot I travel, but go ahead,
The dare I took, and uncertainty shed.

A walk so forlorn, a walk so lone.
A place we are, together alone.

ACROSTIC POEM
My Twilight

Shadowed in the twilight, her name echoes bloom.
A fearless mother, who carried me once in the womb.
Nevertheless, my compass for someone so stern,
Desiring relaxed, like flames that burn,
Heartfelt love, generously given away,
Yearns for her son to spread his wings and fly high.
Around she will remain to flutter, reborn a butterfly.

BEAUTY LIES IN THE EYE OF THE BEHOLDER

Who Only Sees the Profound
Is beauty conditional, subjective or objective?
Does it have to be nostalgic, symmetrical, or pleasing to the
eye?
Perceptions that differ with questionable opinions,
To what the eye perceives as either pleasing or plain.
Meanings of beauty seem different to one another,

But it is what lies deep within that is of utter ferocity.
To catch sight of does not need a set of conditions.
To call something beautiful it need not be perfect.
Be it a bouquet of flowers or a heap of filth,
Every creation has a lacking to be imperfect,
Is Where its lies, Where its lies.

Taking hold of a rather subjective form,
People have contrasting understandings of beauty.
The escapade may well do numerous to people unalike.
May move someone's heart, may narrate a lengthy story,
May evoke nostalgia, may make someone cognize.
One that is capable of yet looked past quite oft.

The eye either judges harshly or appreciates boundlessly.
It takes on the character of its master, the beholder.
The beholder stands there still, musingly staring.
Where the mind contemplates, but the truth lies,
Nothing is beautiful, nothing is ugly,
Everything depends on how we see everything.

We can never envisage what beauty is to be.
Bar creations of the almighty respected with devotion.
In scattered works where it resides deep at the core.
When scrutinized, deciphered without prejudice,
And fathom its true glamour in simple words.
But bringing fascination in complex emotions.

The cover of a book is not to be judged, which may deceive.
But what is written inside, where all the hidden qualities hide.
To each their own, everyone has their own tastes.
The feeling of aesthetic solely in the mind of the beheld,
An illusion taking one to squint closely, uncover the unknown,
Taking out the lens of bias, allure seen by those intrigued and
fair.

A DREAM THAT IS YET TO BE DREAMT

As I lie in my swaying hammock, and set sight onto the skies,
A sea of dreams courses through my flooded reflections.
An assemblage out of the blue kindle me of afflatus cries,
Pondering deeply upon my yearns and ambitions.

Dreams already dreamt, but still yet to dream,
With much to do and much to see, I make my way,
Life that goes on lively along an emotional stream,
Aspire till I reach up among the other stars, far away.

Restless, I long to dream more and pace further ahead.
Take me further, for I am still yet to dream.

The gentle breeze strokes, but having been said,
Forgotten discontent, with what is left I deem.

Dreams already dreamt, but still yet more to dream,
With that matters to me, discern what's forth,
Awaken from my slumber, I arise to remain foreseen,
Assuage those thirsty itches, to settle what's hope worth.

A CONCRETE POEM

Kinetic clouds

NILAM SINGH

ONCE WHILE I WAS WALKING ALONE

I walk alone amongst the crowd.
My heart still bleeding, pounding loud.
Through darkened streets, I walk alone.
I have no one to call my own.
I need someone to ease the pain.
To stop these tears that fall like rain.
Alone I walk.
To myself I talk
My Tears tear apart.

"My broken heart"

STEIN JACQUES SHINE - 10A

ONCE WHILE I WAS WALKING ALONE SOLILOQUY

I was walking alone,
enticed by the tone,
of a lapwing bird,
crooning a melody unheard,
to its companion far away,
wishing that it would stay,
I called out,
and the melody drowned,
engulfed in misery,
I presumed my soliloquy.

TRIJAL MAHARASHI -10N

ONCE WHILE I WAS WALKING ALONE

When I was walking alone,
I kept thinking that this behavior of nature seems a bit
different.

Free roaming bumblebees,
beautiful butterflies, redness of flowers deepening in
small plants, as they were saying how beautiful and
unprecedented nature is.

Its beauty was shaking my loneliness a bit,
and asking whether walking alone is a
worthwhile experience or walking the path of solitude is a
constant experience.

There are some untouched aspects of life
which are paved only on the path of
loneliness.

When we walk alone,
 the depth of our thinking is at its peak and strengthens our
sense of loneliness.

When I was walking alone,
 I saw energy circulating around me and felt that energy.
was motivating me to move forward on the path of life.

It is automatically taking me from darkness to light,
telling me this while I was
Walking alone keep calm and carry on.
Keep walking alone.

MOTHER

A mother's love, a precious gem
A guiding light, a shining hem
A heart that beats, a soul that cares.
A love that never fades, never wears

A mother's arms, a safe embrace.
A shelter from life's stormy race
A place of comfort, a place of rest
A harbor for the troubled guest

A mother's voice, a soothing balm
A melody that brings us calm
A source of wisdom, a source of grace
A beacon in life's darkest space

A mother's love, a priceless treasure
A bond that lasts beyond all measure
A gift from God, a sacred flame
A mother's love, forever the same.

SANJAY ADDEPALLI -10H

ONCE WHILE I WAS WALKING ALONE

Alone I was walking with rage,
Toward the ocean, my cherished domain
As my life turns a new page,
And the echoes of insult began to wane.

I looked back at the blackened sky,
Watching as the storm clouds rolled by,
The treasures deep in my heart mold,
A shield strong, with a message bold.

The sounds around me reinforce,
As the cold breeze anguishs many,
The blue lifeline begins a new course,
As different birds chirp in dissonance.

The hurricane's uncontrolled power prepared to wage war,
With all its might ready to uproot the feeble.
But the vow I swore,
Never to fall on the blow it seeks.

Despite the storm and its deadly might,
Despite the impending doom in sight,
Despite the chaos and disaster in store,
An open door awaits us to freedom.
Only the one strongest in heart, is truly free of doom.

A DREAM THAT IS YET TO BE DREAMT
Dream into the sky

A dream that has yet to be dreamt,
A beacon of pure light in the depths of night,
Humanity's hope, a mission to the world,
Advancing far beyond our present sight.

A dream, elusive but yearned for still,
A vision of unity amid rivalries intense,
green and grey converge,
And history renounces its red recompense.

A dream of improbable positivity,
Defying the brink of extinction,
An extension of human capability,
Innovations breaking all known heights.

A dream I wish to happen,
While watching the masses engulfed in peril,
Millions in the epicenter of a multi-rage world.
All I yearn for this home,
Is to remain a blazing light, from deepest of shadows.

YUAN SETHI - 10K

ACROSTIC POEM
Blessing In Disguise

Sincere serene smile brightening up my day,
Hands uplifting me when skies turn gray,
Every hug transmitting warmth worth gold,
Laughter filling my soul, never grows old,
Love you unleash, boosts me to thrive,
Youthfulness brings delight to my life.

Majestic is your maternal love, enables me to win,
Only one with me through thick and thin,
Tucked me in with your work-worn hand,
Holding me always, you unwaveringly stand.
Ever-present lighthouse shining the beacon that leads.
Radiating positivity that satiates all my needs.

BEAUTY LIES IN THE EYES OF THE BEHOLDER

Beauty isn't defined by definitions,
But by the diverse observations.
Some it does please,
While others ignore it like a breeze.

Like a painting on a canvas,
When strokes of colors multiply.
Some find it captivating,
Others might find it awry.

So different is every soul,
Beauty's perception knows no control.
In the eye of the beholder, it will inhabit,
A puzzle of viewpoints, fitting bit by bit.

For the beauty of a garden,
Flourishing with diverse bloom.
Each perspective is a petal,
Contributing to the full bloom

AYHAN MOHAMMED - 10A

ONCE WHILE I WAS WALKING ALONE
Solitude's Serenade

When I was walking alone,
The world was mine to roam.
My thoughts were free to roam as well,
And with each step, a story to tell.

I walked along the winding path,
With no particular destination in mind.
The journey, not the destination,
That was all that I hoped to find.

CHRISWILL GRACIAS - 9D

ONCE I WAS WALKING ALONE
Thoughts on a Dark Path

I was walking alone,
On the path to my home,
Holding the groceries in my hand,
Till I reached my land,

The moon's light,
Which shone on me bright,
Like the superstar in the shows,
Looked by everyone who knows,

The people in the dark,
Just as eerie as the dog bark,
Look at me in the eye,
As if I told a lie,

The feeling was straight,
Just like my mother, holding my fate
When I do a crime,
Wasting her time,

Alas, I see a gate,
The freedom from this fate,
I look at my journey,
When I hear a rather familiar sound saying
Wake up, honey!'

ACROSTIC POEM
My Small Angel

Sweet and small beauty
Identical version of me
Sunshine, that helps me to grow.
Talented and a true friend
Elegant, a waiver of hope
Rattling snake, still fighting over a bar of soap

BEAUTY LIES IN THE EYE OF THE BEHOLDER
A Clear Glass

Beauty is something you can see or hear,
A beautiful gift seen by your eyes or heard by your ears,
One may be pessimistic, others optimistic,
Each one defines unique characteristics,

So how do we explain beauty,
Surely, it's not our duty,
Is there a right or a wrong?
To whom or what does it really belong?

A person can't be same,
Each of them looks differently towards a bee in their lane,
Some say ahh! Others say woah!
That's the perspective of nature we sow,

The taste of beauty is diverse,
Maybe it changes in each and every multiverse,
We all have different perceptions,
Of many clean and clear conceptions,

The true meaning of beauty we cannot teach,
It's not something we can preach,
It's not like paper we can store in a folder,
Because beauty lies in the eyes of the beholder.

A DREAM THAT IS YET TO BE DREAMT
DREAM BOX

Dreams are for all,
Some dreams with great glory, others in which we fall,
Love for dreaming is one we all share,
Vivid and lucid ones have their own fare,

Some dreams last a night,
Others we try to accomplish with all our might,
Dreams give us great ambition,
To reach a beautiful transition,

Our life is made up of dreams,
Each a path of different streams,
For if our dreams die,
We shall wander like a bird with no wings to fly,

A dream that has yet to be dreamt,
A unique mystery in the present,
Future that will unfold,
Like dreams have foretold.

CONCRETE POETRY
MY UMBILICAL CORD

My
family is my
big bond. A place
where each and everyone
fond. The connection of each
and everyone never bends. Even if
broken, always mends.   In time of need
my family will help me succeed.   Somehow
always there, a family who will mourn and care. A place
of   people who are our own, will help when   ever
we are alone. My family is just like a book,
but once I take another look, their love is
always near , even though the ending is
unclear.   I love my family a lot ,   still we
fight like snots. Their love is the purest I
can get, I still owe them my debt.   The
family who held   my hand when I was
scared,   my sister who I fought because
I wanted candy that I should have shared.
My family is the greatest gift, maybe time
for me to get of the lift. I Love My Family!

KHUBAIB AMEENUDDIN - 9A

ONCE WHILE I WAS WALKING ALONE

Once while I was walking alone,
Through the remnants of a city unknown.
Where dark clouds obscured the light,
And all life seemed ravaged in sight.
Amidst this land of despair,
Stood high a solitary tree.
Its branches being the lone hope,
For the future none could foresee.
As I stood there transfixed,
Halted in my journey of seclusion,
I glimpsed the growth of saplings betwixt,
Ready to aid the tree in time of strife,
Proving that one is never alone in the journey of life.

ACROSTIC POEM

Uplifting attitude that motivated me
Soothed me and proved to be.
A beacon of hope in my challenges
Intelligent eyes that only see the beauty of people
Diligent personality that always helps the shy and feeble

MOHAMMED ZISHAN SHANAVAS - 9A

ONCE WHILE I WAS WALKING ALONE

Once while I was walking alone,
Through the forest of the unknown.
I thought to myself,
What could lie in this delph.

As I walked further,
I saw an animal in slumber.
How I wish that could be me,
As peaceful as the creature seemed to be.

But alas, I must continue on,
And stay strong.
This journey will not be easy,
But I will keep moving, and not get queasy.

The world nowadays is so fast paced,
With only some of our goals being chased.
This is the harsh reality,
And that's causing so much anxiety.

We forget to appreciate the wonders of life,
As we struggle through each day's strife.
I wish life could be simple,
Where everyone could watch the stars twinkle.

83

ACROSTIC POEM

Bold and dauntless, you illuminate my way.
Radiating kindness, your light never fades.
Open-hearted, you offer unwavering support.
Thank you for always being by my side.
Honesty and sincerity, your words resonate.
Empathy and guidance, you've seen me through.
Radiating goodness, shining pure and bright.

CHAITYA SHAH - 9H

ONCE WHILE I WAS WALKING ALONE

Once, while I was walking alone,
in the viridescent grass sown,
I heard a whizzing noise,
Straight down the impasse,

This made me befuddle,
knowing that I should match,
so, I went ahead finding a bache,
and what I found, was truly staggering,

For, it was a little fauna,
with a severe looking trauma,
I felt a little resolute,
and so, I took it to my residence

During its therapeutic process,
I could see a lambency in her peeper,
it was a puny kitty,
who needed to be reclaimed,

In the end, I could notice something,
and that was the grin of my quaker (kitten)
it also made me realize that,
A small lend always helps in its prosperity

NEIL MACHADO- 9A

ONCE WHILE I WAS WALKING ALONE

Once I was walking alone,
In a cold, deserted street.
Where streetlight didn't show the direction,
A leaf, a twig or even a tree.

Moving along for I had no idea,
If I was right or wrong.
Didn't know what lay up front,
It can just be a giant hole.

No signs of cars, no sign of birds,
Not even a noise from the distant woods.
I walked along, 1 know God's by my side,
Yet I am scared cause of the road at my side.

When I walked, I saw a creature,
In a book did it feature
Curiously, I tried to reach her.
But 'Wake Up', said my teacher!

AARON THOMAS - 9A

ONCE WHILE I WAS WALKING ALONE

Once I was walking down the street,
And I saw a man with shoes on his feet,
But they were on the wrong way round,
And I couldn't help but laugh out loud.

I pointed it out and he looked down,
Realizing his mistake with a frown,
He quickly switched them to the right,
And walked away, out of my sight.

But I couldn't stop laughing for a while,
And people around me gave me a smile,
I guess it was a funny sight to see,
A man with shoes wrong, just like me.

Lesson learned, I must admit,
Double-check my shoes before I commit,
To walking out into the world each day,
And avoid being the next shoe display.

MOHAMMED YUSUF- 9D

ONCE WHILE I WAS WALKING ALONE

The Golden Bird
Once while I was walking alone,
Through the creepy woods of darkness,
I came across, a rather unfamiliar tone,
Though it left me perplexed,
I was for sure, that that tone wasn't monstrous.

It was quite bizarre,
To hear a charming voice of melody,
To hear a sign of hope,
To hear a voice that strived to be heard,
Amid the melancholy darkness of the woods.

As I tip - toed my way across the endless woods,
Making sure, not to be spotted by our common foes,
I traversed across, in search of that voice,
That was as mellifluous,
As the songs played by Beethoven.

With every ounce of my energy left,
I persevered my way through the woods,
Like how a brave bear would,
I searched around for paw-prints or bird feathers,
Like a detective, yet none found.

After a considerable amount of time,
when all hope was about to be lost,
I heard the very sound, I had heard in the beginning,
With every step taken ahead, the sound started to grow,
A couple of short steps; I believed I had reached.

I saw it perching on a tree branch, singing its unique melody,
It didn't take me long enough, to recognize that it was
A Golden Bird, that was as bright as the moon,
A Golden Bird, that shone bright across the creepy woods,
A Golden Bird, that symbolized hopes and aspirations.

Symbolizing life, was it, the Golden Bird,
That emerged bright amongst the darkness,
Like a beacon of hope through the pitch - black skies,
Proving to the naysayers that nothing is impossible,
Even for a little bird that strived to be noticed by the world!

ACROSTIC POEM

First to accompany me, in times of grief and despair,
Repairing wounds of desolation and dejection,
In time, my friend, we shall be as inseparable as magnets,
Ensemble, my friend, we shall explore the seven seas,
Neither shall we separate nor shall we wrangle,
Did I mention that that friend, is also my best friend??????

BEAUTY LIES IN THE EYES OF THE BEHOLDER

The way we perceive things in our lives,
Paves the way for our success,
Our thoughts and actions are influenced,
Not by others. but by the way our mind perceives things.
so, remember, be unique, and perceive things in your way.

The way different people perceive things may vary.
So, one need not bother. on what others may think.
If we train our minds to perceive things in a positive way.
Even a failed light bulb may provide inspiration.
To a great scientist. to try again. even if it takes 2774 tries!

One man's trash is another man's treasure,
Just comes to show that perception changes everything,
The way we see things in our life.
Really shapes who we become,
So just remember, beauty always lies in the eye of the
beholder!

ERIC IMMANUEL - 9D

ONCE WHILE I WAS WALKING ALONE

While I was alone,
Alone in the gloomy streets, I went,
When my soul longed for light,
I cannot find it that night,
Into the dept of unknown,
While I was alone
As I travelled further into the streets,
I felt nudged,
A Nudge I felt in my heart,
My soul to fall apart,
Lost in darkness, I had to atone,
While I was Alone
At the darkest of hour,
I felt lost in despair,
Many people were there,
But they stayed in the dark without care,
I stood there all alone,
While I was Alone
It made no sense,
My destination was not here,
So, I ran from the dark gloomy street,
As fast as I can with my feet,
With determination and faith, I reached a new zone,
And now I was not Alone,

Many people gathered around me,
As I told my story,
Now I felt this was my destiny,
A town of light and tranquility,
And at last, I was home,
Where I was not alone.

ACROSTIC POEM
MY BROTHER

Born to be my friend,
Radiant as a beam of light.
Outgoing lad with a social blend,
Thriving with a smile so bright.
Helpful sometimes, naughty other times,
Evan, is his name, my partner in crime,
Reliable partner and my little brother.

SHAURYA ARJUN GUDIKANDULA - 9A

ONCE WHILE I WAS WALKING ALONE

Once I was walking alone
while using my favorite cologne.
Thousands of thoughts going through my mind like a cyclone,
Those thoughts made me realize if I was alone.

As I was walking down the path which looked completely
unknown,
I felt my heart completely shattered and torn.
The stars in the sky made me realize I wasn't alone,
They hypnotized me into thinking they were following along.

The path looked dark and outgrown, which made me feel left
out.
But the moon and stars made me neglect it.
Even when we think we are alone, there is always someone
for us.
These thoughts made me realize If I was really alone.

ALAN SCHUMI - 9G

ONCE WHILE I WAS WALKING ALONE

Once I was walking alone,
in a garden full of flowers, which were all grown,
a place where I think I am on a throne,
or a home, a place where I belong.

A garden where my mind is at peace,
This fact is the truth, to say the least.
The flowers are all in full blossom,
like a country that just gained its freedom.

Then I heard something called an echo,
The flowers are happy with me, I guess so.
These all happened on their own,
that faithful day I was walking alone.

ACROSTIC POEM

Some days ago, I had a dream,
People say that the past is the past, but that dream was one
that was supreme.
Echoing down my body like a shiver,
Can anyone tell me why I am feeling bitterness flowing down
my spine like a river?
I am telling you, this one is deep.
A wave of pain, like a load I can't keep
Like someone I know who is special and who appears to me in
my sleep.

A DREAM THAT IS YET TO BE DREAMT

Life ends when you stop dreaming.
Your dreams go on till you accomplish it.
All we do is dream of creating,
Until you stop dreaming and life ends with it.

Life goes on depending on your dream,
You believe in the dream, and you are a team,
The terror and pain of accomplishing that dream,
Will be giving you a good gift to redeem.

All the ambition is a result of our dream,
Just like how cake is a result of whipped cream.
All our ambitions are yet to be achieved.
Like how there are dreams yet to be dreamed.

95

CONCRETE POETRY

Something which goes in a loop but doesn't mean it is the same yet, we waste it.
We use it but we don't really know or even notice it being wasted. All we do
is lazing around. But we all forget the fact that the time we waste will
never ever be back, as wasted time will be the past. If more people
can realise that we can all invest this time in stopping these
damn problem like global warming and poverty then
maybe, just maybe, we can solve this problem
and make the world a safe, secure
and sustainable pl-
ace to live in not only for
us but also for our future genera-
tions. the time we use will make us all
Live a happy and peaceful life. Consider time
as money, we can invest money. It can either give
You make a profit or a loss. Time is quite similar. Just
like money, we can invest our time in something and by pro-
bability, we either succeed or we fail. That means we can have a
loss in time or get something more in that time like achieving a goal of
yours. This is why people say that time is money and we should not waste it.
Because the thing you waste will never be repeated. It will be useless and we will
never get it back. You only live once, so use the time in your life for something useful.

KHAWYAN SOLAI CHELLAPPAN - 9L

ONCE WHILE I WAS WALKING ALONE

Once while I was walking alone,
I pondered on the benefits of being alone,
Reflecting and comparing both sides,
And discovered how it could enhance our lives,

Being alone per se appears to be tedious and eventually boring,
But a blend of solo and socializing is soaring,
How is solitude beneficial?" You ask me!
I haven't intended isolation rather time alone, don't you see?

You and l, we need a break.
from our hectic schedules, it's no mistake.
Just strolling alone in the woods,
Unravelling God's handiwork, filled with goods.

This is a time leaving beside our daily duties,
Spending hours gazing at nature's beauty,
After doing so I nonchalantly end this time,
Heading home with another rhyme.

SHAYAN NOUSHAD - 8 I

ACROSTIC POEM

Poured with unconditional love, they stand,
Affectionate souls, a guiding hand.
Revealing strength in every stride,
Eternal pillars, side by side.
Navigating life's uncertain lanes,
Teaching lessons that forever remain.
Sharing wisdom, nurturing our dreams.
Protectors of our tender hearts,
A sanctuary from life's alarms.
Devoted mentors, strong and true,
Inspiring us to be our best, too.
Poured with unconditional love, they stand,
Affectionate souls, a guiding hand.
Navigating life's uncertain lanes,
Teaching lessons that forever remain.

A DREAM THAT IS YET TO BE DREAMT

In the realm of whispers and shadows cast,
Where dreams unfurl, their secrets vast,
There lies a vision, untouched, unseen,
A dream that floats in realms serene.
A tapestry woven with threads unknown,
A melody played on strings unsown,
A vision painted in hues untamed,
A symphony untamed, unnamed.
In realms uncharted, it quietly stirs,
A dream untethered by earthly blurs,
A dance of stars on the velvet night,
Igniting hope, sparking eternal light.
This dream resides beyond the sight,
In a realm where time takes flight,
Where boundaries fade, and souls take flight,
In the canvas of dreams, pure and bright.
Unfettered by doubts or mortal fears,
This dream awaits, beyond the years,
A masterpiece yearning to be seen,
A vision locked in the vast unseen.
In hearts it lingers, a gentle plea,
To manifest in reality,
To shape the world in its sacred art,
And awaken dreams in every heart.
So, close your eyes, embrace the night,
Unleash the dream, let it take flight,
For within you lie the power to be,
The dream that has yet to be dreamt, set free.

POEM TO MY PAST SELF

To My Past Self, I Send a Note
Oh, younger me, with curious eyes,
Unveiling wonders, chasing blue skies,
I pen these lines to reach your core,
A time-traveling message, to the days of yore.

Fear not the shadows, hold onto dreams,
For life's symphony awaits, or so it seems.
Embrace the unknown, take leaps of faith,
In every stumble, discover strength's true face.
Cherish the moments, both big and small,

For time's swift passage will soon befall.
Let laughter echo, let tears cleanse the soul.
In every chapter, write your story whole.
Seek not perfection, for it's a fleeting guide,
Instead, let authenticity be your pride.

Embrace your quirks, let them unfurl,
For they shape the canvas of this precious world.
Oh, dear past self, with youth in bloom,
May these words guide you through the gloom.
Know that within you, resilience thrives,

And your spirit, in every moment, strives.
So, step forward boldly, and embrace the quest,
For you hold the power to be your very best
As time unfolds its mysterious dance,
Embrace the journey, take a chance.

CLERIHEW!

There once was a man named Jack,
Whose fashion sense was a bit off track.
He wore mismatched socks with pride,
And claimed it was a trend worldwide!

His pants were never quite the right length,
His shirts were often a mismatched strength.
But Jack just shrugged and said with glee,
"I'm a walking fashion catastrophe!"

His hat collection was truly bizarre,
From sombreros to a Viking horned czar.
He'd wear them all with a mischievous grin,
Causing quite the fashion faux pas within.

Jack's style was an enigma, no doubt,
People stared, some whispered, others would shout.
But deep down, Jack was proud to be unique,
Fashion norms were something he'd never seek.

So, here's to Jack, the style trailblazer,
In his world, fashion rules were just a teaser.
He taught us all to embrace our own flair,
And never be afraid to stand out and share!

A MISTAKE I'D LIKE TO REPEAT!

In the depths of my memory, it lies,
A mistake I'd like to repeat, I surmise.
A moment of folly, a chance not taken,
An enchanting dream I wish I hadn't forsaken.

In the haze of time's relentless flight,
A choice made wrong, against what felt right.
Oh, how I yearn to rewind that day,
To mend the past and find a way.

It was a fleeting moment, an ephemeral glance,
Yet, it left an indelible mark, a lingering dance.
Regret now gnaws, like a persistent ache,
A haunting echo, with each step I take.

The path not chosen beckons still,
A road less traveled, a whispering thrill.
What if I'd embraced that leap of faith,
And cast away the shackles of my wraith?

But life's a canvas, brushed with mistake,
Each stroke, a lesson, learned for love's sake.
And though I stumble, I'm not confined,
For in the errors, growth I find.

So, I'll cherish the errs, and the lessons they teach,
For they've shaped the soul that's within my reach.

Yet, deep inside, a desire remains,
To repeat that mistake, break free from chains.

For sometimes, a mistake can be a serenade,
An ode to the heart, a melody never fades.
And if given a chance to rewrite history,
I'd embrace that mistake, unshackling mystery.

But alas, time's river flows just one way,
And we must move forward, come what may.
So, I'll carry this memory with bittersweet delight,
A mistake I'd like to repeat, in the realm of night.

NEW FORM OF POETRY
Synopsis:

This form of poetry is an immersion into twilight's celestial palette, where stars bestow their enigmatic secrets upon an unfolding narrative. Within this canvas, a garden of intricate thoughts blooms, each line a petal bearing metaphors and dreams. Guided by the hand of rhythm, emotions flow like rivers, weaving a lyrical odyssey through the undulating landscapes of existence. With a delicate touch, the verses peel back the layers of the heart, revealing its most intricate patterns. The resulting poetic tapestry captures life's essence, with verses and stanzas interwoven to create a rich mosaic of the human experience.

Twilight's Canvas

Amid twilight's canvas, stars converse in whispers,
A tale spun anew, as the universe glimmers.
In this sacred garden of thoughts and musings,
Each petal unfurls, secrets gently oozing.

Metaphors and dreams intertwine like vines,
Painting emotions with rhythmic lines.
Life's river, guided by a skillful hand,
Flows through each verse, as time's grains expand.

Through highs and lows, a lyrical journey we take,
In this poetry's embrace, emotions awake.
Heart's portrait emerges, stroke by stroke,
A tapestry of existence, a profound yoke.

Verses and stanzas, like threads they combine,
Capturing life's essence, a symphony divine.
This form, expansive yet meticulously refined,
Unveils the human soul, each layer entwined.

NEW FORM OF POETRY
SOUL ECHO POETRY

In the realm where dreams embrace,
Where stars cascade with gentle grace,
Soul Echo whispers tales untold,
In verses woven, mysteries unfold.

Each stanza, a reflection deep,
In thoughts and feelings, secrets keep,
Words like tendrils, reaching wide,
Across emotions, they gently glide.

Metaphors dance in twilight's glow,
Emotions bloom, like flowers grow,
Rhymes and rhythms, heartbeats entwined,
Soul Echo's song, a symphony refined.

Through valleys of longing, mountains of hope,
In the tapestry of words, we elope,
With every line, a connection's birth,
Soul Echo's magic, echoing worth.

So let the verses paint your skies,
With vibrant hues that mesmerize,
In this new form, emotions flow,
Soul Echo's poetry, a journey to bestow.

ABHIRAAM RENIL - 7C

ACROSTIC POEM

Hailing from a world of beauty and grace,
Incredibly talented, with a smile on her face,
Mastering life with intelligence and wit,
A true wonder, a rare gem

EVAN JACOB – 7C

ACROSTIC POEM

Marvelously
Overflowing with love
And
Touching the
Heart of
Everyone she
Reaches

SIBTAIN BHIMANI – 7D

ACROSTIC POEM

My Mom
Strong in all the work she does
Understanding all my problems
Kindness all around her
Knowledge a source of information
Always there to help me
You are blessed to have me.
Nurturing a love that never ends
A true friend

ETHAN SERMON GHOSH 6 – I

ONCE WHILE I WAS WALKING ALONE

Once, while walking alone, my steps embraced solitude's song,
A path uncharted, where reflections danced along.
Silent whispers of nature caressed my wandering soul,
As the world around me found solace in the shadows' console.
Sunlight painted my spirit with warmth and light,
Whispering trees and blooming flowers ignited my sight.
In that solitary stroll, I discovered an inner tone.
 A symphony of self, a serenade of my own.

ACROSTIC POEM

Fearless protector, always by my side
Advice and guidance, you never hide.
Teaching me the strength, to face every stride.
Honoring your love, with deep pride
Encouraging, nurturing, my constant guide
Reliable, dependable, my father, my pride

POEM TO FUTURE SELF

In shadows of today,
I glimpse my future self,
A tapestry woven with dreams and unknown wealth.
With bolder steps and purpose unfurled,
I'll navigate the labyrinth, a transformed world.
Time's patient sculptor, shaping what will be,
My future self-beckons, awaiting me.

SIVABALAN - 6A

A MISTAKE I'D LIKE TO REPEAT

A mistake I would like to repeat.
is keeping a whoopee cushion under my father's seat.
I'll wait for my father; I'll wait and watch.
I'll wait for the whoopee cushion to give its amazing launch.
Oh, it's so funny, Oh it's so rib-tickling!
The sound it gives out is so amusing.
Then soon he will put his punishment mode on max.
because now I know that his humor lacks
I would like to repeat this mistake.
because this big risk I'm happy to take
(I don't even think this is a mistake! Do you?)

MOHAMMAD AFFAN - 6D

ACROSTIC POEM
MOTHER

M-Mummy is full of zeal.
O-0n always working mode.
T-Taking all the tasks hand to hand.
H-Has a multitasking behavior
E-Every time worrying about my future.
R-Responds to everything I ask her.

MESSAGE TO FUTURE/PAST SELF

When I was small, I always played pretend,
But then I thought about having an imaginary friend.
Who can play and talk and write and draw,
Who can turn into animals and shake his paw.

Who can be beside me when no one else is,
Who can keep me company and buy me gifts.
I could make him a friend and a foe,
He can fight beside me and sacrifice his dough.

In my free time we can do prank wars,
Or read books or imagine flying to Mars.
This might get over when I'm more mature,
But having an imaginary friend is all I adore

RITVIK BHARGAVA – 6D

ACROSTIC POEM
A simple thought

Education on safety while being online.
Stop using random sources.
Activate different protections against attackers
For safety use different passwords everywhere
Enter in the technological world being prudent
Transact using verified devices.
Youth need to be educated about this.

POEM TO FUTURE SELF

Dear future self
There was a candle in my heart, ready to be kindled,
There was a void in my soul, ready to be filled,
Did u get some of things?
I have been longing for,
Answers, to my the never ending why,
Why I'm following old patterns and the like.
Playing in imaginative world thinking
That it will be same in the life journey.
My future self is with full of love and life,
I'm grateful for what I have been,
And excited for all that will be right.
I am free to be myself, and that is all I need to win.

GURUCHARAN KARTHIK -6N

POEM TO FUTURE SELF
Big Boy Gurucharan!

 I will be a big boy,
Never play with a small toy!
The higher class I go,
Harder and harder your journey grow

Life is not that easy,
Difficulties make you glossy!
Being away from home is not great.
It's hard like doing a skate!

Feel that you are confident,
World around you will compliment!
No problem for having a beard,
But make sure you are being heard.
Be always thankful to God,
Your proud heart will applaud!

JOHAN LIJO JOHN - 6H

CLERIHEW!
COLONEL TOD ASTROPHILE

Good old Colonel Tod Astrophile,
Was a man who never had a smile.
When the skies turn dark and the stars outshine,
He laughs at the sky and wakes Frankenstein.

KRISHAB RAKESH - 6I

ONCE WHILE I WAS WALKING ALONE VERSION 1

Once while I was walking alone,
I went into an antique shop zone.
There was a magical book which caught my eye.
That was trying to fly high to reach the sky.
I took it home to see what it can actually do,
I asked, "Can you only fly or do more?", hoping for a different view.
"l can talk, laugh and show you the world", it said,
And page by pages, it showed a lot on a spread.
The book helped me in my work at school,
We both started to ascend with cool.
We both became good thick friends,
Becoming inseparable like paper and pen.
But one day we had a terrible fight,
Which made him sad and out of my sight.
I missed him badly as days passed,
Searching him badly and found at last.
Stuck ribbon to a rod, all night along,
Freed him and said "Sorry" for all the wrong.
I took him with me happy days turned out.
And happily, our friendship tree sprout.

ONCE WHILE I WAS WALKING ALONE VERSION 2

Once while I was walking alone,
I thought everyone walks their own path known.
They had their companion, pets, or friend,
But me alone don't know when it will end.
My legs are paining after each and every step,
Then there was someone standing to help.
Finally, I have a friend at its best,
Thank God! I feel very blessed.
We walked North, South, East, and West,
Playing and had fun fully messed.
Suddenly he was nowhere to be found,
He left me alone without any sound.
I thought what was wrong with me,
Was I acting dumb, stupid, or sounded crazy?
But I decided to leave all negative emotions now,
And think always positive, I took a vow.
I could see my path nice and clear now,
I thought how did it turned up so easy, how?
Then I knew there was something missing around,
Happiness is that something which can be found.

ACROSTIC POEM

Many words are there to describe you,
Outstanding, kind, loving and caring are few.
Talented, thoughtful, beautiful, you are,
Happiness hover around you like a shining star.
Every day you make me feel loved and special,
Relying on you at each and every level.
Thank you, mom, for being my strong pillar,
From the bottom of my heart to the moon and stellar.

POEM TO MY FUTURE SELF

Hey hi!! Hello or should I say hey bro,
Or would you have other slang which I won't know.
It's so strange talking to future self as you,
Because I know there will be changes in looks too.
I know that the future world will be changed,
But for you it will be okay and quite engaged.
I can just imagine, the future world could be,
Flying cars, AI robots, everything beyond we see.
I wonder what I have finally become,
A police or doctor or king owning a kingdom.
Or did I become something which I never dreamt,
But something which I really wanted to be meant.
Hey bro, a little advice from the past you,
Follow your dreams and live happily through.
Enjoy the small moments with your family,
Be good always and make sweet memory.

A DREAM THAT IS YET TO BE DREAMT

A dream that has yet to be dreamt,
I am trying to understand what it really meant.
Is it the famous inventions that people made,
Or the natural calamities that caused place to fade.
Will it be about myself, being a giant and alone,
With robot malfunctioning and humans gone.
Will it be about me fighting a war in the past,
Or enjoying with Elon Musk in the space aircraft.
Thinking about success, many things and goal,
Comes like a dream which you can only control.
Dream is not the thing that you see in sleep,
But that doesn't let you sleep, and you take a leap.
When likes and wants are yet to be met,
A dream is there that has yet to be dreamt.

JAHAN ASOODANI – 6I

ONCE WHILE I WAS WALKING ALONE

Once while I was walking alone,
I realized, how much I was in pain.
As my love all in vain
So easy to hide the tears roll down in rain.
The memories we had.
The love we shared.
And how much we cared.
With each and every step I took
It became painful for me to look.
That there were laughter and tears down the years
It all blew off in the fears.
But nothing we love is meant to last.
So now I have learnt to keep walking alone.

ACROSTIC POEM

S- Secret keeping
l- Impulse giggling, hugs, and kissing
S- scene creating, always fighting.
T- Together trouble facing
E- Ever lasting.
R — Real love

A POEM TO MY FUTURE SELF

To my future self - Live again
In life, there will be people who hurt you,
Spend more time with those who love you.
you may lose people you love.
Pour that love on people who need it.
Take your troubles best you can.
Stand right up and face it like a man.
Work for a cause, not for applause
And live life to express, not to impress.
As we are hurt by crimes
But healed through times.
So, forget the rest, just be your best.

ABOUT THE AUTHOR

Heikin Ashi Trader is recognized worldwide as the specialist in scalping with the Heikin Ashi chart. He has been trading this way for 19 years. He traded for a hedge fund and then went into business for himself as a trader. His scalping book "Scalping is Fun!" is an international bestseller and has been sold more than 30,000 times. You can find more information about his scalping method on his website www.heikinashitrader.net